INSIDE
THE WALL

INSIDE
THE WALL

by Don Crawford

Tyndale House Publishers
Wheaton, Illinois

Coverdale House Publishers Ltd.
London, England

Library of Congress Catalog Card Number 72-97650
ISBN 8423-1650-7

Copyright © 1973 Tyndale House Publishers,
Wheaton, Illinois

First printing, April 1973

Printed in the United States of America

CONTENTS

For my two saintly mothers—
one gained by birth,
the other by marriage—
both of whom taught me much about
   abiding in the Lord

FOREWORD
A Crack in the Wall

Timothy Yu sat in his publishers office in Hong Kong, talking about recent events in China. Having spent years studying the mainland from Hong Kong — ever since he was forced from his homeland at the 1949 Communist take-over — Yu's opinions, I knew, would be those of a seasoned observer. He could give me the latest word on the exciting possibilities of Chinese evangelism in the wake of China's celebrated diplomatic thaw.

Yu soon dampened my enthusiasm. "China's present policy of allowing a limited number of foreign visitors to Peking and other cities should not be taken as a change in its basic attitude toward the West. The welcome will be restricted to a selected few whose visits are expected to serve China."

The reopening of China, Yu indicated, will occur only after China's internal struggle is resolved and the leaders see no danger of losing their hard-earned political power and economic control.

I wondered if Yu's quarter century of observation and literature production would attain its great goal. "Oh, China will open again," he asserted. "But change comes slowly in China."

The small door that promises entry to China's 800 million people has apparently only been cracked. But through this slit flows hope for renewed proclamation of the gospel.

In anticipating Christian ministries in China, a vital question must be confronted: What is the current religious status of the Chinese people? While in Hong Kong I tried to determine the effectiveness of China's infamous Cultural Revolution — those chaotic years of 1966-68 when Mao-worshiping youths zealously trampled the traditions of the past. By talking to refugees and people with Chinese contacts, I had to accept the truth that open worship, except by compromising groups, is virtually nonexistent in today's mainland China. The twenty-year imprisonment of the dynamic Christian pastor Watchman Nee, until his reported death in 1972, has become a legendary example of Communist suppression of religious freedom. But in my search I discovered as well the indomitability of Christians' faith. The authentic case histories that follow demonstrate God's sovereignty and mercy in Communist China.

To protect family members and friends still living in China, the names and locations mentioned in the accounts have in many cases been disguised. Otherwise, however, the information is set down as it was given me by the individuals themselves.

I am indebted to Edvard Torjesen, Radio Taiwan representative with The Evangelical Alliance Mission (TEAM), for his review of the manuscript. Torjesen's understanding of the situation in China, which proved particularly helpful in the preparation of the manuscript, is based on a lifetime association. Born in China of Norwegian missionary parents, he received his education in that country as well as in the United States and Canada. In 1948 he went to Mongolia as a missionary for TEAM, a service that was cut short the following year because of Communist pressure. From 1949 to 1951 he served in Hong Kong, and most of the subsequent years in Taiwan.

The enlightening Afterword by Arthur Glasser, former missionary to China and dean of the School of World Missions at Fuller Theological Seminary, is reprinted from *Eternity* magazine by the kind permission of the Evangelical Foundation.

Don Crawford
Carol Stream, Illinois

1 Forbidden Fellowship

Mei-ling doesn't fit the part of a daring adventurer. The heroine in adventure stories is supposed to be young, slender, and slinky. By contrast, Mei-ling is short, plump, and over sixty. But her frequent sojourns into Communist China have nonetheless been filled with excitement and intrigue.

Mei-ling is able to make regular trips to China to visit a younger crippled sister because her papers are in order. Not being a refugee (since she moved to Hong Kong before the Communist take-over), she — and her Western money and goods — are welcome. Her adventure starts as she crosses the border. She must leave the mixed passenger, livestock, and freight train that takes her from Hong Kong and walk across the railroad bridge that spans the narrow river separating the British crown colony from mainland China. Before continuing her journey on the train, after it crosses the bridge without its human passengers, Mei-ling must take her turn in one of the border station's "dark rooms."

In this room she has to strip and open her bags for a thorough search of everything she is taking into China. If everything seems satisfactory, she is given a slip of paper which lists her name, destination, length of stay, and the goods and money she is bringing in. It is a simple but vital document. "Your life depends on this piece of paper," Mei-ling told me. "If you stay longer than the paper says, you're in trouble. If you lose the paper, you can't return."

So precious is the document in the eyes of the Chinese government that the bearer isn't even trusted with it. As soon as Mei-ling reaches her destination — no matter what time of day or night — she must take the document to local officials who exchange it for an identification card. Why so much attention to the paper? "To keep someone from stealing it and using it to escape to Hong Kong." The all-important piece of paper is returned at the end of the stay.

Mei-ling's visits have always been punctuated with praises for Chairman Mao. It begins at the border crossing. After leaving the "dark room," visitors must sit in a waiting room facing a large plaque inscribed with the sayings of Mao. Upon the command of an official, the group stands, right arms raised, to repeat the leader's paeans. Anyone who does not do so enthusiastically is taken to another room. What happens there? "I don't know," Mei-ling confessed. "I always shout my 'praises' and I've never been there."

Praises have rung out for Mao even when visiting a restaurant, Mei-ling reported. Eating out, apparently, is an adventure in itself. A large crowd is always waiting to get into the eating places. When the doors are finally opened, there is a rush for tables. Those who don't get one stand behind those who do. But soon all are standing as the headwaiter signals with the clap of his hands and everyone rises to sing a martial tune.

It is in the daily routine of the Chinese citizens that the attention to the government leader becomes overbearing. Although the situation now seems to be easing, those not excused because of work or sickness have had to spend up to ten hours a day in "confession" sessions. The clockwork regimentation of the Mao-thought meetings went from 8:00 A.M. till noon, from 2:00 to 4:00 P.M. and from 8:00 P.M. till midnight during Mei-ling's visit. If one works all day, he must go to the nighttime meetings, she was told. Mei-ling's brother-in-law, too old to work, had to spend his days at the meetings. This gave him little time for food buying. And shopping was not a satisfactory excuse for missing a meeting, even though that in itself was a time-consuming business.

Getting in the meat line at 3:00 A.M., as many others also tried, gave the old man no assurance that his individual allotment of pork — a few ounces every ten days — would be obtained. The same was true of cloth for clothing, rationed at five feet per year, which Mei-ling described as "rotten." Mei-ling's gifts of food and clothing were keenly appreciated.

The oppression of the people, Mei-ling believes, is maintained through fear — and cunning. Mei-ling knew of many families that had been separated by one of the government's favorite ploys:

"They can send citizens anywhere they want to," she told me. "Often it is to the fields to work, usually at the home of their ancestors. This way they break up families." Once moved by the government, the people are seldom allowed to return to their homes. Mei-ling told of one young mother who was sent to help on the farm and had to leave her baby with its father. Then the father was sent to work in the fields and the baby had to be cared for by whoever would take it. "If someone refuses to go where the government tells him to," Mei-ling asserted, "he is sent to jail to be brainwashed." Or worse. She has seen people tied to trees, legs and arms stretched taut in four directions, for their disobedience.

Mei-ling has observed the constant struggle for political power — which, like hunger, has been a part of Chinese history much longer than the current Communist regime — add to the woes of the people. "They have riots in Canton all the time," she explained. She herself was once caught between an anti-Mao faction and government troops. "I ran and prayed as the shells whined around me," she related.

Her older sister was an early victim of the civil strife. Traveling from one town to another with her six-month-old son and a sixteen-year-old nephew, Mei-ling's sister was stopped by guerrillas who demanded her money. After she had given them all she had, they demanded still more. Unable to render any, she was beaten and forced to eat human excrement. The ordeal caused her death. Her nephew brought the infant and the story of her suffering to Mei-ling's younger sister, who cared for the boy until he was taken into the army at the age of eleven. He was later killed in one of the frequent flare-ups.

In an apparent attempt to muster the loyalty of the people, Radio Peking — which comprises a network of stations spanning the huge country — constantly urges the people to get ready for war, reportedly imminent though no enemy is ever cited. To lend realism to the appeal, bomb shelters have been dug in all the homes, Mei-ling reported. One evening she was discussing the war preparations with friends in her sister's home. During the conversation she exclaimed, "The world is getting worse and the Lord will come back very soon. If you don't believe in the Lord, you're in trouble!"

She realized the indelicacy of the statement when she saw the look of horror it produced on the faces of everyone else in the room. In strong whispers she was told to never say anything like that again or her friends would all be "cleansed." The way they uttered the word, Mei-ling knew it must be something horrible. Worse, they might lose their identification cards, which were needed for purchasing food and clothing.

When I asked if there was any hope at all in the situation, Mei-ling described the riskiest —

and yet the most promising — adventure she had experienced in China.

During the Cultural Revolution, Red Guards entered every home, took all the books they could find, and burned them, but a neighbor of Mei-ling's sister was able to hide a Bible. It is being read today in defiance of a government order banning the reading of anything other than Mao-approved books. No one ever tells where the Bible is located, of course. Only the owner knows who else reads it. But singly, each at an appointed time, every Christian in the neighborhood has an opportunity to read from it.

And in spite of the seditiousness of listening to anything but Mao-approved thought on the radio, Mei-ling has joined her sister in turning down the radio, inserting an earplug, and together listening to comforting words of Scripture, encouraging assurances of prayer, and soul-reviving hymn singing coming to them from the Far East Broadcasting Company station in Manila.

There have been enough examples for them to know the danger in their action, but it is a risk they gladly take to keep faith alive.

2 P.S. I Love You

Like many refugees in Hong Kong, Martin Lu has a strong desire to return to China. In addition to a spiritual yearning to take the gospel to his people, Lu's reasons are intensely personal. He left a wife and four children in China when he came to Hong Kong in 1948.

Lu thought the separation would be for a couple of years — while he attended a seminary — but then the Communists gained control of the mainland. In their exchange of letters Lu's wife encouraged him to stay in Hong Kong "until things get better." So far, the dream of going home remains unfulfilled, not only for Martin Lu but for the many in Hong Kong who have been separated from their families in China.

The decision to stay in Hong Kong was a painful one. Lu could have gone back to China — on the Communists' terms. But since the Communists weren't lavishing love on people like himself who were the product of Western missions, the terms were harsh. Four who graduated from the seminary a year ahead of Lu went back to China and none was given the freedom to preach. Lu learned their fate from a missionary who came out of China after they had returned. One was harassed to the point of committing suicide. One was sent to prison where he died. Another was imprisoned for three years and then sent to Peking for prolonged "special instruction." The fourth's whereabouts became unknown after he, too, was condemned as a spy. Lu knew he would be far better able to support his family from Hong Kong than he would from a prison cell.

As Pastor Lu talked about the years of separation from his family — his children ranged in age from eight years to three months when he left China at the age of twenty-eight — I realized that, in addition to the characteristic oriental stoicism he possessed, he relied on an extra measure of grace, not just to survive but to become a productive worker in God's kingdom.

Ironically, it was because of his dedication that he was given the opportunity to go to Hong Kong. He was teaching at a middle school and preaching for three congregations when he was selected by his church body's general office for the seminary training. He knew from the lay leadership which had developed in his congregations that they would be able to carry on in his absence. He still believes that the groups are faithful to their Lord although open worship has been stopped. Many of his parishioners had gone through temporal hardships before, he told me. Prior to the Communist take-over, they had experienced the World War II occupation of China by Japan. Lu's own Christian commitment had been settled in this period. He was married in 1941 after his graduation from high school and was teaching school some distance from his home town when he gained "a very strong faith." When his father died in 1944, he had to travel through Japanese posts to visit his family. "I felt God would protect me," Lu recalls, "and he really did. I met many enemies along the way, but they didn't hurt me." After the war he took on the responsibility of the three congregations.

Although separated from his home since 1948, Pastor Lu has been able to "see" the changing situation in China, thanks to his wife's faithful correspondence. At first she was able to express freely her trust in God, but as the government became stricter she was forced to use subtler means to let her husband know she continues in the faith. In one letter she put in large characters on the first page: "We hope you come back to help establish our new country." But later in the letter she said, "If you have our Father's work to do in Hong Kong, do it." He knew she had been forced to write the first sentence.

When Mao-thought meetings were inaugurated, Mrs. Lu wrote about her evenings spent quoting Chairman Mao or learning new Maoisms. An important part of the meetings, she revealed, is a "cleansing" session when transgressions are confessed. At the sessions Mrs. Lu is required to read her husband's letters. After one meeting she wrote her husband: "Your letters get very good credits because you ask the children to obey the government. But, one thing: you should not mention any religion to your children. This is prohibited. Your children have freedom to choose their own faith. From now on please do not mention any religion in your letters."

Realizing his wife had written the letter because of the pressure she was under, Pastor Lu stopped making direct references to his own sustaining faith. It was another matter he would have to place in God's hands.

But this was not a new experience for him.

In the early years of the Communist regime the people in Mrs. Lu's area were placed in communes. The men were in one camp, the women in another, and the children in yet another place. Lu learned then to trust God to do what he couldn't. He is satisfied that, in spite of the handicaps under which his wife has had to work with them, all of his children are faithful Christians. They've found ways to tell their father so. He knows that because of their faith, their life has not been easy.

When the oldest son missed a Communist youth meeting, for example, his offense was reported by classmates. It was two years before Pastor Lu learned what happened to his son. Lu's wife wrote merely that the boy would be taking "special education" for two years and would not be able to write. But after he was released, Lu's son wrote him a long letter. In it he said, "I do not care if someone censors this letter and puts me into prison again. I want you to know the truth. The cicadas here still have their freedom to sing, but I cannot say what I want to say. All the flowers have their own names, but people like to add special names to each one. If they could talk, they would say, 'No, I don't want this name.' I have a name which I do not want. . . . The small animals can still enjoy their mother's love, but I can't. I want to tell you that I now believe that the One who is above us still takes care of us. He is the only one who can give me comfort." Surprisingly, the message came through uncensored — either passed over by a sympathetic official or the poetic language misunderstood by a careless one — to bring joy to a father's heart.

Since his imprisonment, life has been even more difficult for Lu's oldest son, through whom the pastor has two grandchildren. The children must live with Lu's wife. "Although my son is now the chief electronics engineer in a northern province," Lu told me, "he doesn't make enough money for clothes." Lu is thankful he can send money to help support his children and grandchildren, whom he may never be able to see. Lu's second son married a university classmate; they have one child and live in Inner Mongolia. His only daughter married a train engineer. Both his daughter and second son live reasonably well by current Chinese standards.

Pastor Lu feels most frustrated about his youngest son, who grew up without paternal influence under a totally Communist educational system, although he is certain his wife has been able to point the boy toward the Christian faith. Lu was encouraged by a Christmas greeting in which his youngest son wrote, "Father, we still wish you a Merry Christmas as we look up to the One above us."

Lu was worried at the start of the Cultural Revolution in 1966 when his son joined the Red Guard movement. Later, however, obedient to his mother's wishes, he dropped out. The move ruined the boy's chances for a higher education, Lu believes, even though educational opportunities seem to be increasing in China now that the devastating Cultural Revolution has been reversed. "My youngest son has had to go to the farm to 'learn something from the farmers,' " Lu told me. According to Mrs. Lu's letters, few escape this type of service. "Even medical doctors are sent to the farm, and my wife writes that it's often hard to find a doctor," Lu revealed.

Pastor Lu pays touching tribute to his wife's ability to carry on her crucial single-parent role under the circumstances of life in China — especially since the family has been placed in a "nonperson" status. He supports her as well as he can through his letters and shipments of money, but the political situation is so unstable that he must send each transmission with a prayer that it won't be misused or misunderstood.

A comment in Lu's letters, acceptable at one time, may at a later date get his wife into trouble. After he had sent greetings from several acquaintances in Hong Kong, for instance, she replied with a request that he no longer mention the names of his friends. The families had become *personae non gratae* and Lu's wife had to deny any knowledge of them.

The money Lu sends his wife receives careful treatment. "It must be placed in the bank," he explained. "When my wife wants to buy things, she must list all the items on paper and show it to the banker. Sometimes the banker says, 'Lady, you'd better not buy too many articles at this time. You must buy this part, and next time you buy the other part. Otherwise, your neighbors will be jealous and they will start to talk against you.' My wife must do as he says."

Not that there's a great deal of choice about what to buy. While the economic picture is apparently improving, rationing must still be practiced in much of China. "During the Japanese occupation people at least had clothes to wear," Pastor Lu remembers. "But not now. If my wife wants to make one garment, she has to save her clothing tickets for a whole year. Each monthly ticket is good for only a few inches of cloth. It takes a year to save enough tickets for one piece of cloth, and then she must sew her own clothes."

Despite the uncertainty of the circumstances his wife faces, Pastor Lu places an abiding trust in God to work things out. He has learned the effectiveness of prayer. When the future seemed especially dark for his eldest son after two years of imprisonment, Lu recalls, the Lord answered his intercessory prayers in an unexpected way. Classmates of his son who had gone on to the university, knowing young Lu had been ostracized and denied a high school diploma, spoke to the university president in his behalf. The president agreed to accept him without a diploma if he could pass the entrance examination, which he was able to do.

Along with the rest of the free world, Pastor Lu is hopeful that the present crack in China's openness to the West may signal a future opportunity to safely enter his homeland again. But he has learned to be patient as he waits for God's clear signal. For the many Chinese in Martin Lu's situation the day of return cannot come too soon.

3 Mao's Book Burners

He had taken the English name of Peter when I met him in Hong Kong. He was taller than the average Chinese. And he was camera-shy. But otherwise he blended into the student population of the high school he was attending. His command of English, for example, was good as was true of most of the students — although Peter had been acquainted with the language only a couple of years. His desire to help mold a better world was not unlike that of his fellow students — or of other young people around the globe, for that matter.

The fact that Peter swam out of mainland China to satisfy his quest did set him apart from many of his contemporaries. Not all, of course, for many Chinese escape to Hong Kong in this fashion. Peter's saga, however, is important because it offers a view of Chinese youth not revealed in the usual portraits of Mao-quoting revolutionaries.

Peter had the "misfortune" of being born to a

landholding family in the early years of the Communist regime. The fact that his parents had been "landlords" — a label as obnoxious in China as "Communist" once was in America — was to plague his early existence. Peter also had the misfortune of being intelligent. He liked school but questioned arbitrary assumptions. "Personal expression is a necessity for a human being," Peter believes. "But in China if you express your own ideas — unless they coincide with Chairman Mao's — you are treated as an anti-revolutionary."

In grade school Peter was considered a model student. He was even made captain of the Pioneers, a Communist-front youth organization. "I can still recite hundreds of Mao's slogans," Peter told me. "In China you saw and heard them everywhere. Everyone quoted them." But Peter could see a disturbing discrepancy between what he was taught at school and what he read in his parents' extensive home library. Other things bothered him, too.

"My grandparents came to Hong Kong after the revolution in 1949," he related. "Grandfather couldn't stay in China because he was a well-known merchant and the Communists hated him. My grandparents always sent us letters and food and clothing. I wondered why such nice things came into China from outside.

"When I was about twelve," Peter recalled, "I decided that if Chairman Mao said something was good, that meant it was probably bad. If he said something was bad, then I would think it might be good." He came to this conclusion alone, for his parents never criticized the government. They did, however, encourage him to read and formulate his own opinions.

"You can't imagine the stupid and foolish things some of our leaders did," Peter told me. "Pictures, magazines, and movies all told us how bad America is. We were told how cruel Western missionaries were — how they robbed the Chinese of their land and culture. Even though I was not a Christian, I doubted the stories. One teacher put up a picture of the President of the United States and said, 'Hit it!' I just couldn't believe that all the things our leaders said were true; that the Western nations were all that bad. I wanted so much to find out what was really happening outside of China."

The disintegration of China's educational system during the anticultural Cultural Revolution spurred this desire. As Red Guard youth, under the blessing of Chairman Mao, roamed the land to destroy all religious and cultural ties to the past, teachers and intellectuals became the subjects of harassment. "The Red Guards might make a teacher kneel down before his class or go barefoot — any number of things — until his self-respect was gone," Peter explained. "Many teachers quit their jobs in disgrace. A lot of them committed suicide. I saw a very prominent professor jump from the fifth floor of a campus building and kill himself. He was not a stupid man. He was a scholar. How sad his heart must have been to do such a thing!"

Peter was only fourteen when he learned first-hand what Mao and the Red Guards thought of "intellectuals," "landlords," and other "antirevolutionaries" who were standing in the way of Communist progress. Peter's father had been removed from his job in a Canton bank and sent to work on a collectivized farm. Alone in the home Peter and his mother were aroused one night by Red Guards who had surrounded the house, shouting revolutionary slogans. The leader forced open the door and several of the young hooligans entered. Peter recognized classmates among the mob. Some of them he had considered good friends. Now in their frenzy they were denouncing Peter and his mother.

"Landlords!"

"Antirevolutionaries!"

One of the youths waved a knife in front of Peter's mother and told her to kneel down. Peter was forced into another room. Other guards ransacked the house. The family's library of books was taken outside and burned.

Accused of being an antirevolutionary, Peter's mother was deprived government recognition and sent north with Peter to her childhood home in Honan Province. Denied registration, Peter's mother was unable to work or even to obtain food, relying on the handouts of former friends to survive.

"This happens in China," Peter said matter-of-factly. "A lot of families have the same situation. Father at a farm and mother living with friends, this month with one family, the next month with another.

"In Honan Province," Peter related, "I practiced my swimming." Through an uncle Peter learned of four young men who were planning to leave China. Just fifteen but large for his age, Peter was permitted to join them.

Pretending to be young peasants heading back to the country to work, the five left a community in Honan by train, transferred to a bus, spent another seven days walking in the mountains by night, hiding in bushes by day. Although rain fell steadily on them the last five days of their journey to the coast, the soaked youths kept on.

When they arrived at the shore, a typhoon was blowing fiercely in from the sea. The group hid in bushes for two days, hoping the wind and rain would abate. On the third night they decided to make the plunge, typhoon or not. Holding hands, their clothing strapped to their backs, they entered the violent waters.

The waves were high and the sound was thunderous, Peter reported, but when they had fought their way some distance from the shore, the sea was calmer. Alternately swimming and resting, always watching for the lights of Hong Kong, the group encouraged each other through the night. At last they saw a light. But as they approached it, they realized it was on a small island. Afraid that it was not safe, the young men changed their course.

A haze of light in the night sky had to be Hong Kong. They swam toward the glow and just before dawn pulled their weary bodies ashore to fall into exhausted sleep.

They hadn't slept long when one of the men woke the others. The youths changed into the clothing they had carried on their backs and set out to find a village. "When we found a village at last and asked the peasants to help us," Peter related, "they refused. The first several families we contacted wouldn't help. But finally a family agreed to help us if we would give them some money, which we didn't have. I promised them I would pay after I found work in Hong Kong. So they said okay and hired a car to take us to Kowloon. The first man I met when we got to town was a policeman. I just froze. I tried to tell myself, 'This is a free land. I don't have to be afraid.' "

But the fear was there, I could tell, even as Peter related the incident. I could see why he had recoiled at my request to take his picture.

Peter gave the officer the name of his grand-mother — his grandfather had died — and was taken to her. Since she had never seen him, she could not identify Peter until she asked several questions about the family. When he answered properly, the old lady beamed. "This is my grandson!"

The first Sunday Peter was in Hong Kong his grandmother, now a Christian, took him to church. It was his introduction to Christ and a new way of life. "Sometimes when you are in a situation where you can't do this and you can't do that," Peter explained, "it's as if your brain is covered. Once you get out, it's like taking a breath of fresh air. It's like being born again."

But Peter doesn't write his beloved homeland off. "Americans need to understand us," he asserted. "We have a beautiful culture and beautiful country — plenty of mountains and lakes. Most of our people are very kind, very hard working, very clever. I think our golden time will come again. I am very confident about the Chinese. Such a great number of people cannot be controlled by so few."

For those who express little concern about governmental philosophies, Peter feels he should ask them to come live in China for a while. "Then they would appreciate their own life. And maybe they would act differently.

"I see things in Hong Kong that make me sad," he added. "Making money is so important to some people. Sometimes I wonder why a man will lie perpetually, slandering and backbiting his fellowman. Why is he unable to see good even in his friends?"

Peter confided that he misses his family very much, but he also told me, "I think my happiest day was the day in Hong Kong when I became a Christian.

"I think people should really understand that hate makes people terrible," Peter said of his experiences in China. "Now I understand the principle of love. This is the only way to overcome hate. I hope that Christianity can return to China and that more people can realize that to accept Jesus Christ is to change their lives."

Although Peter possesses a strong desire to see America and many other places in the world, his main hope is to go back home. Why? "There are so many people in China who don't know Jesus Christ."

4 China Calling Dr. Ho

For Dr. Tom Ho, getting out of China seemed an impossible dream. But after nearly two decades of praying for it, he saw that dream become reality. The long-delayed expatriate insists that God lives in Communist China. In fact, that's where he found the Lord.

Dr. Ho's family had moved from Shanghai to Singapore in 1948, a year before the Communist take-over, while he was still in high school. Tom stayed behind to complete his studies at the church-supported boarding school he attended. Then came the change of government and for six months he was unable to communicate with his parents. In the letters that finally reached him, Tom's folks urged their son to make application to join them. They were certain he would have no trouble getting a passport and a visa to Singapore since the family had come out of the country quite legally.

When he made application, however, Tom was told: "You're a student! You shouldn't leave your country." When the youth insisted that he wanted very much to join his family, the official concluded the conversation with what Tom later learned was a lie: "Even if you were able to go to Singapore, the government there would refuse to let you enter. They arrest everyone who comes from China." Dejectedly, Tom returned to his room to write his parents the sad news.

As often as he could, Tom visited an aunt and uncle who lived in the area. But most of the time he was desolate. He didn't get much sympathy from his teachers, concerned as they were about the future of the school, except for his English teacher. A highly independent American, Miss Dennis seemed determined to serve the students as long as she was able. She did not disguise the fact that she placed her trust in God, for which Tom admired her, even though he was not a Christian. In his distress, however, he found himself praying, "If there is a God, please let me pass through this terrible situation."

Not long after his prayer of despair, he accepted an invitation to attend a Bible class in Miss Dennis's home. Among the students in the informal class, Tom felt free to reveal his frustrated desire to leave China and join his family. Through the careful instruction of Miss Dennis and the confident example set by the Christian students Tom learned to place his trust in God no matter what he might face in life. Early in 1950 he made a public confession of faith in Christ and was baptized. Shortly thereafter Miss Dennis was forced to leave the country.

After graduating from high school, Tom was selected by the government to attend medical school. He would have preferred joining his parents, but when he applied again for a passport he was told once more that he could not leave his country, to whom he owed his first allegiance. At the university medical school Tom discovered a surprisingly large body of Christians. "At least ten percent of the students were believers," Dr. Ho told me, "and at a time when it wasn't expedient. Some of the outspoken Christians were denied degrees."

But it was a time of growth for the reluctant medical student. "We had a true student fellowship," Dr. Ho remembers. "There was no missionary or minister to give us guidance. But we loved each other and we always prayed and sang together. If one of our group was getting low marks, we would give him extra help. If someone was discouraged, we would pray for him.

"I think because we all knew that things were not going to be easy for us, we determined to strengthen each other. There was in fact a small revival at our university right after the Communist take-over. Twice a year all the Christian students would come together for special meetings — once in the summer and once in the winter. Two thousand were in attendance the last time we got together, in 1954, but the authorities were so alarmed at the size of the group they outlawed the meetings altogether."

After 1955, the year he began his hospital internship, Tom saw an increasing antagonism toward Christian activity by the government. Christian interns found little chance to witness openly of their faith, other than through their concern for the patients. Dr. Ho recalls one rare opportunity to deal with a patient, a youthful Communist with terminal cancer. "Before he died," Dr. Ho believes, "he knew the Lord Jesus."

After his internship Dr. Ho was sent to a government hospital in North China, where he missed the Christian fellowship he had known at the university. "Public worship at a local church was nothing but a mockery," he told me. "As much obeisance was paid to Chairman Mao as to God. It was obvious who dictated the order of worship. In fact, a government permit was required before anyone could preach. And this permit had to be obtained each week. There was someone at every service to check on this and to make sure the government and the Communist Party got their share of the praise.

"We lived and worked in such an atmosphere of suspicion I seldom had a chance to add a spiritual depth to my medical practice — although I was aware of the need." The doctors were quartered three to a room with at least one of each trio a member of the Communist Party. It was risky to express one's faith. Dr. Ho was never able to read his Bible openly. "If a Christian encountered someone he thought might be a fellow believer, he had to be very careful because some people pretended to be Christians just to get us into trouble," Dr. Ho explained. "If you harbored 'wrong' thoughts, it was reported to the government."

But in spite of all the surveillance, Christians could identify one another. One evening, Dr. Ho recalled, he was preparing to bathe when he heard a newly-assigned doctor, presuming he was alone in the shower room, raise his voice in the melody of a familiar hymn. "You'll never know how joyously I joined the new man in humming, 'Holy, Holy, Holy! Lord God Almighty,'" Dr. Ho related. "We didn't dare sing the words, but we both rejoiced at this unexpected fellowship." The two were able later to get away from the city and on a lonely hillside share their faith and sing and pray together. Occasionally, when they were in their quarters alone, they were able to communicate in low voices. One time they tuned the radio to a Far East Broadcasting Company station and were listening to sacred music when their Communist roommate entered.

"That's nice music," he said.

"Yes, it is," the young doctor replied calmly as he switched stations.

Such close calls made Dr. Ho's Christian walk largely a solitary one. He remembers especially one night when he was walking in the garden of the hospital. "It was so quiet. Most of the patients were sleeping. No one else was in the garden. A verse from Deuteronomy came to me then: 'As thy days, so shall thy strength be.' That promise gave me the courage to face the lonely days ahead."

There were to be many of them. It wasn't until the mid-1960s that Dr. Ho was presented with an opportunity to try again to leave China legally. In a letter from his mother he learned that his father was quite ill. She urged her son to join the family in Singapore. Dr. Ho asked for permission to make the visit. His request was denied. As his father's condition worsened Dr. Ho made repeated applications to go to Singapore. They were repeatedly denied. The elder Ho lingered four years in a vain hope that he might see his son again.

When his father died, Dr. Ho again requested permission to go to his family. Again he was refused. Resigning himself to the apparent fact that nothing would persuade the authorities to change their minds, the doctor tried to forget his disappointment in his devotion to his work. Inexplicably, six months later, he was told that he could visit his mother if she would come to Hong Kong.

In a poignant final meeting before his trip to Hong Kong Dr. Ho could say only "good-bye" to his Christian companion, for their Communist comrade was also present. Their unspoken prayers bridged the communication barrier, however. Both knew the journey would be one way. So as not to arouse suspicion, Dr. Ho took only a few belongings, leaving his books and most of his personal possessions behind.

His passage to freedom was not to be easily gained. He was held up at the border station because he had no visa to enter Hong Kong. He had heard of people being detained as long as two months on this technicality. So, as many before him had done, Dr. Ho found lodging in a small inn near the train station and waited. The days stretched into weeks, the weeks into months.

One month. Two months. Three months. Still no visa.

"Every day I was afraid the government would send me back to the hospital," Dr. Ho related. In his letters to his mother, who was staying with relatives in Hong Kong, he tried not to reveal the uncertainties that entered his mind. "But I wondered if the rumor that Hong Kong would not accept any more visitors was factual. Every time I looked through my window and saw someone enter the hotel, I wondered if that person was bringing me word about my visa. But every day it was nothing. Always nothing. I had to pray for my sanity."

Then he started getting visitors he wished would leave him alone. People who were supposed to be representing past aquaintances offered to get him into Hong Kong extralegally if he were willing to pay the money — always exorbitant — for clandestine passage. He refused, and prayed more fervently as he waited it out.

In the fourth month of his despairing vigil, Dr. Ho was informed by an authoritative visitor that his visa was waiting for him in Shanghai. He wrote a hurried letter to his mother and bought a ticket north. The train to Shanghai plodded, but it was better than another day in that inn. With his precious visa in his possession at last, Dr. Ho returned to the border station, patiently endured the thorough search of his luggage, and finally stepped aboard the train to Hong Kong. "I breathed freely for the first time in four months. Coming to Hong Kong seemed a miracle."

The first thing he did after leaving the train was to embrace his mother, who had been meeting every arrival since she had received her son's letter. The second thing he did in the British crown colony was to request political asylum. Dr. Ho is now a productive citizen of Hong Kong. He remembers the Christians in China in frequent intercessory prayer and supports a radio ministry into China. These are not merely benevolent gestures. He *knows* Christ's church is living there.

5 Brothers and Strangers

What a difference a few years can make.

When Kim Sung swam to Hong Kong from China in the mid-1960s he sought free expression of his Christian faith. When his younger brother Kwan followed his exit, swimming out in the 1970s, he came claiming no faith at all.

As their stories unfolded, I wondered how two brothers could have so many common experiences and yet be so different in their philosophical stances. The difference could only be attributed to the drastic change that engulfed China after the Communist take-over. Kim had been reared in a Christian atmosphere before the change in government. Kwan had been reared communally on a steady diet of Communist doctrine. Yet Kim and Kwan share a Christian heritage. Their grandfather had accepted the faith and passed it on to his children. Kim told me he grew up "imbued with Christianity."

Kim was seven years old when the Communists took control in China, and the Sung family, once respected landlords, became the target of government attacks. The infant Kwan did not witness, as Kim did, their grandmother's humiliation. Though past sixty, she was hung by her thumbs and beaten until the rope holding her broke and she dropped, mercifully fainting, to the ground.

Kim observed the many changes in the school system that had become accepted procedure by the time Kwan turned school age. "We started having four hours of Communist doctrine each week — an hour a day four days a week — and sometimes more," Kim explained. "We were often told how very, very good Communism is. Later, in high school we had a time once a week when we were to reveal our thoughts. Some of us confessed we didn't believe in Communism, which meant we could hold no hope for higher education." As a Christian, Kim also faced unemployment after his graduation from high school. In his discouragement, he determined to escape to Hong Kong. He soon learned how difficult it was to accomplish that desire.

Inexperienced in such a clandestine operation, Kim was promptly caught by border guards and taken to a concentration camp. He was thoroughly frightened and humiliated. "I could not keep from crying," Kim recalled. He quickly discovered, however, that his frustration was not unique. Twenty or more newly captured escapees joined them every day. All were assigned to hard labor and given only a little bit of rice and a few tiny salted fish to eat.

Then one night Kim's troubled sleep was disturbed by someone whispering urgently for him to escape. Half awake, he rushed out of the open prison door — into a fusillade of gun shots. Instinctively Kim dived for the ground. A strong gust of wind caught him and rolled him over and over. A typhoon was battering the coastal area. "I simply could not stand and could hardly move an inch," Kim remembered. "All I could do was stand still and be captured." Taken with the other prisoners to a vehicle station, Kim was ordered to squat down.

"I told myself that should we be taken back to our home town the consequence would be unthinkable," Kim related. This thought gave him the courage to run. The guard shouted at him to stop and fired his gun. Kim kept running. "But my legs were too heavy to obey my will. I could scarcely lift them."

A huge prison guard caught up with Kim and grabbed his arm. He raised his gun at Kim's head and a shot burst forth. Kim fell limp to the ground. When he came to, he ran his fingers over his head and found a big lump — but no blood. The guard had hit his head with the handle of the gun as he pulled the trigger.

Kim was dragged back to the other prisoners where he was tied so securely he could not move. "This was an experience I've never had before," Kim recalled. "Very soon the blood in my hands seemed to coagulate and I lost feeling in them." In the car that took the escapees back to the concentration camp someone quietly untied the rope binding Kim. "Otherwise, I'm sure I would have lost both my hands."

Sent back to his family, Kim did not give up his determination to leave China. He was soon revising his escape plan, this time in greater detail. Early on an April morning in 1964 Kim left home without informing his family. If he were caught, they could not be involved. A friend living near the border took him in. "We knew there were many guard stations near the border," Kim related. "And we knew there were watch dogs. This time my escape route was a three-mile stretch of sea."

Kim had grown up on the coast and was used to swimming in the ocean. But the conditions were vastly different now. It was a dark night. The water was cold and threatening. There could be no turning back. As Kim and his friend neared the deserted shore, a figure suddenly darted along the beach. The two tensed, scarcely breathing. The figure disappeared into the darkness. Was it a border guard? Had they been spotted? Kim didn't want to wait and see. Trotting as quietly as he could, he reached the shore, quickly stripped to his dungaree shorts, and slipped into the chilly water. In his pocket, carefully wrapped in plastic, was his New Testament. "But," Kim confessed in relating the incident, "at the moment I wasn't even thinking about God. And his chastening was almost immediate."

The chosen route was an oyster bed with many sand banks that Kim had to climb over. Whenever he put his feet down, they would be sucked into the mud and sand. When he pulled them back out, the oyster shells cut his flesh. "I felt as if I were walking on a hill of knives," Kim said. *"Then* I asked for God's help, as I should have done at the outset. When I turned to God, I regained strength and continued on."

Twice during the seven-hour journey Kim was seized with cramps. "God gave me strength and calmness," Kim related. He turned over and massaged his legs while swimming on his back. And God brought him to Hong Kong, where he found sympathetic help. He enrolled in a seminary and is now the pastor of a Swatowese congregation.

Kwan's life in Communist China differed considerably from his brother's. Separated from his parents in a communal situation, he was indoctrinated in Communism throughout his school years. A teen-ager at the advent of the Cultural Revolution, Kwan joined the thousands swelling the ranks of the Red Guard youth movement. "It was great while it lasted," Kwan told me. "We could go into anybody's home. Nobody could stop us from taking anything we wanted — watches, rings, books for burning." The Red Guards were able to travel anywhere they wished on any train and eat at any restaurant without charge. The red band on their arms was their license to get food or shelter — or search libraries and homes for antirevolutionary literature. Huge bonfires of confiscated material became the symbol of their crusade. People yielded to the demands not so much from a fear of the youths — although the Red Guards carried guns and knives as part of their uniforms — as from a fear of the government which supported the movement.

"Mao was our god," the youth reported. "We all had pictures of him in our homes. We all carried his little red book. We all shouted — and believed — his quotations."

The Red Guard action seems particularly incredible for an ancient nation with a tradition of respect for elders. "That was the point of the Cultural Revolution," Kim told me. "To destroy the old culture, the old customs. Before, children were expected to obey their parents and respect their teachers. But this was an 'old custom' and therefore to be abandoned." The young people didn't need their parents as they once did, for they might be raised in a commune, he explained. The Red Guards were fed by their victims and trained by the army. They could always get something to eat, always find a place to stay.

Teachers who tried to apply the old rules were objects of ridicule and maltreatment. "One teacher had her hair cut like a mop and her scalp painted and was made to run through the city without shoes. Many teachers were so humiliated and disgraced they killed themselves," Kwan reported.

Mao had barely launched the Cultural Revolution before he realized it was a mistake, but the rampaging youth were harder to turn off than to turn on. Late in 1968 Mao directed the army to crack down. Most of the youths were sent to work on collectivized farms. This was such a departure from the wild, free life they had known that for many Chinese youth the Mao idol toppled. Kwan expressed his own disillusionment:

"On the rice farm where I was placed, all the work was done by hand. We were busy seven days a week from five in the morning until six at night — with only an hour out for rest and lunch. We had little to eat. Sometimes we ate the raw rice without vegetables or meat. After twelve hours of work we were all ready to sleep at night, but the lice and bugs kept us awake. For 'recreation' we held discussions about the benefits of Communism. Of course, for the farmer, Communism had meaning. Farmers and laborers probably fare better than they did before the Communists took over. But most of us lost our lust for Communism right there."

Like his brother Kim — and thousands of other disappointed youth — Kwan decided to get out by swimming to Hong Kong.

After my interview with the Sung brothers, I reflected for some time on the differences between the two. I was disturbed that conditions of life in China had been altered in the brief period of time that separated their ages to the extent that a child of the revolution could have his family faith obliterated. For Kwan claimed no allegiance to any religion (although Kim hoped to change that situation through his own witness). But there is this obvious truth in the situation: Even though the Communists in China have been successful in temporarily chaining the minds of some of the Chinese people, extreme dissatisfaction nevertheless exists.

Kwan is but one example of the thousands of disillusioned youth who are seeking a better life by fleeing China. As they come to freedom, the refugees usually come into contact — directly or indirectly — with Christianity. And it is the evangelized refugee who is the most likely candidate for taking the gospel to a reopened China.

6 Hope in Hong Kong

"Almost every family in Hong Kong has someone back in China," a Kowloon businessman told me. The statement is believable, considering the fact that 90 percent of Hong Kong's four million residents have come from China since the Communists took control of the mainland in 1949. These 3,500,000 Chinese expatriates profoundly affect the economy of the British crown colony. They also represent a current challenge to Christian missions and a future hope for the evangelization of their homeland.

When one ponders the strategic location of Hong Kong, he can only marvel at the miracle of its existence. It would seem a choice plum ripe for picking by the giant on whose borderline it rests. Thanks to a large work force accepting low wages, and one of the world's largest natural harbors, Hong Kong has become an industrial power. Its industries have zoomed from a few hundred factories in 1945 to currently over five thousand. Its spinning mills are among the best in the world. Its booming electronics industry is successfully competing with established world leaders. Its attraction to tourists can be appreciated in the $29,000,000 spent there annually just by American visitors.

Surprisingly, with all its desirable assets, Hong Kong is not molested by China — although it is virtually defenseless. In the words of the Kowloon businessman, "A phone call is all it would take to have the British give up Hong Kong. For if Mao wanted it, he could certainly have it." But as it is, the free port on her doorstep is also an asset to China. Hong Kong provides mainland China with an outlet to the world — and offers the world an inlet to China. It is a valuable marketplace. Half of the food eaten in Hong Kong is supplied by China. Huge Communist stores and banks in Hong Kong reach tourists and traders from around the globe. So China has been content to let Hong Kong remain, even though as an escape hatch for millions of dissatisfied Chinese citizens it represents an embarrassing propaganda disaster.

The Chinese refugees have in turn presented Hong Kong with a formidable housing problem. While Hong Kong's land area covers nearly four hundred square miles, most of the immigrants have squeezed into only sixty-two of those square miles and have made the three-mile-square city of Kowloon, with its nearly one million people, one of the most densely-inhabited spots on the face of the earth. Along with Kowloon, nearby Hong Kong Island, on which the colonial capitol of Victoria is located, and suburban New Kowloon contain much of Hong Kong's population. The largest political segment of the colony, the 355-square-mile New Territories adjacent to mainland China, is the least populated, possibly — along with economic and geographic reasons — because Great Britain's 99-year lease on the area expires in 1997, at which time it will revert to China.

The concentration of people in the Victoria-Kowloon area has provided a continuing challenge to government and benevolent agencies. Christian groups have also stepped in to help provide medical, educational, and occupational assistance for the many destitute refugees. Because a myriad of needs are being attacked, there is perhaps no "typical" Hong Kong mission work. But an excellent capsule of how just one of the many evangelical organizations working in Hong Kong has been facing the always-changing situation was presented in the December 1971 *China-Hong Kong Tidings* published by the Christian and Missionary Alliance:

> From its inception in 1958, the rooftop school/church plan of the CMA was to be a self-supporting project. The mission built the simple structures, after which each school was responsible to raise teachers' salaries and other overheads from tuition charged. The intent of this plan was to use the facilities on the weeknights and weekends as a

center of evangelism. By 1960 the CMA had four such schools operated by pastors of churches that came into existence by means of the roof-top school.

Soon the number of immigrants and births raced toward a staggering figure, calling for newer types of buildings tailored around the most ambitious governmental resettlement scheme the world has known. . . . [In the mid-1960s] housing facilities introduced by the government called for a separate six-story school building constructed as a part of a resettlement estate complex. Known as "annex schools," it was to revolutionize the church/school program instituted nearly ten years previously.

To be sure, this enormous pilot plan provided more space and accommodated nearly 2,000 students as compared to 500 in the roof-top variety; but the prospects of operating such a big school was also a financial impossibility. Yet, as usual, the Lord was one step ahead, and in 1966 an unusual opportunity was presented to the CMA to operate one of these schools. . . . The CMA Church Union (national church) now runs thirty-two Sunday schools, with 3,400 students, and seventeen secular or other type schools with 7,000 primary and 1,300 preparatory students — all directly under the gospel's influence.

Now a new program offers free government education on the primary level, thus working a hardship for our existing roof-top schools that have no financial support above and beyond the limited tuition fund. (When the children are able to attend a school without the need of paying tuition, then our schools which charge tuition find their students shifting to a government-supported or subsidized school.) For this reason we urge you to specifically pray that pastors feed their hungry sheep in a way that will stimulate energetic church growth. This will enable the roof-top churches to locate in newer premises, retaining the essential center of evangelism.

It is this emphasis on evangelism among the numerous evangelical groups in Hong Kong that is getting the gospel of Christ into the hearts of the refugees — and thus paving the way for eventual outreach into China. I had an opportunity to talk at length with a product of this peculiar Hong Kong evangelism — Mary Woo, a smiling resettlement dweller who had responded to the ministry of Church Union Pastor Wong, himself a refugee. As I sat in the claustrophobically-small eight-foot-square room which was home to a family of five, I wondered how people could stand to live so close together. From outside came the ear-hammering noise of thousands of children and fellow occupants of resettlement apartments clustered about. My ears were not accustomed to the constant din that reverberated between and through the many buildings. I looked at my beaming hostess and pondered how anyone could exist — let alone smile — under such circumstances. Her "home" was in one of the old seven-tiered "H" buildings — the arms of the H holding apartments opening off a common balcony to the outside and the central crossbar containing communal washing and toilet facilities. These were built in the early 1960s before the sixteen-story high rises with individual plumbing were introduced.

Through my interpreter I learned that there were reasons, very good ones, for the lady's smile. As crowded as these quarters were, she had known worse. After she came to Hong Kong in 1957 to join her husband, the couple lived in a hillside squatter's shack. The floor of their unheated home was made of cement blocks. Rough plank walls through which one open window had been cut, supported a sheet-tin roof. Whenever the rain beat raucously on the roof, everything inside got soaked. Their possessions were few: a table, a kerosene cookstove, and several small benches. Their bed was made each night by placing boards across the benches. Water was at the bottom of the hill, as was the public bath house. As if her living conditions weren't bad enough, Mrs. Woo was married to a man addicted to carousing and gambling. His wage as a clerk in one of Hong Kong's many small market stalls was meager before he regularly squandered most of it in a hopeless quest for an ever-elusive fortune. Quarreling was their constant routine. Nevertheless, two children were born to them during their four-year stay in their rustic home.

Late in 1960 the family was resettled by the Hong Kong government. When the Woos moved into their new home, it seemed luxurious, even though they still had a ways to walk for water and bathroom visits. Another child was born to them, but their happiness was far from complete. Their quarrels seemed to get worse and the older children were incorrigibly wayward despite their frequent whippings.

Then one day a neighbor invited the Woos to a church service conducted by Pastor Wong at the school on the apartment rooftop. Mr. Woo excused himself but Mrs. Woo attended out of courtesy and for the first time in her life heard the message of Christ. If what she heard about his bringing peace was true, she wanted to learn more about him. She couldn't deny that her neighbor who confessed faith in Christ seemed truly happy despite their common plight. She returned to the services and welcomed Pastor Wong's visits. Convinced of her personal need, she accepted the salvation that Jesus offers. As she learned to trust him for daily guidance and found comfort and instruction in reading the Bible portions

Pastor Wong gave her, she found the peace Christ promised.

As Mary became less irritable, her children seemed less headstrong. Her husband, however, responded to her transformation with intensified misconduct. Mary kept from berating him, though, instead praying that her husband would come to share her faith. She was thankful for the fellowship of the rooftop congregation during this particularly trying test of her new-found faith.

Pastor Wong was able to make friends with Mr. Woo, who agreed to let the children attend the church-sponsored rooftop school. But the man's lifestyle remained unaffected. At New Year's time — important to the Chinese as a family celebration — Woo was gone for two days. Mary felt the old frustrations and anger returning as she waited and wondered about her husband's fate. "In my heart I was very much afraid and I became very impatient," she confessed in our interview. "But on the second night, instead of worrying, I attended the church in order to hear the words of the Lord. When I came back home, I was no longer angry." The change in his wife finally had its effect on Mr. Woo. After three years of her patient prayers in his behalf, he agreed to attend a service with her. He, too, came to realize that the emptiness in his life could be filled only by God.

Mary Woo smiled more broadly as she talked about the dramatic change that came over the entire family when her husband finally accepted Christ as his Savior. His gambling ceased immediately, and the family was able to improve their living standard, although their income remained slender. "But now we are happy," Mrs. Woo said simply. Their happiest moments, she told me, are found in reading their Bible together. Yet they have a longing in their hearts. They want to return to China to bring the gospel to their families there.

The most effective evangelization of China, once it fully opens, may well come from people like the Woos, who, as millions of other Hong Kong dwellers, have someone back in China.

7 Leap over the Wall

Would they make it, they wondered. The daylight hours were fading, and the final government deadline was fast approaching. An impossible amount of work still had to be done before the Far East Broadcasting Company could begin transmitting the message of God's love over radio waves to the Orient. The crew worked feverishly. They knew the Lord had pulled them out of "hopeless" predicaments before, but this was crucial. If DZAS Manila did not go on the air that very evening, FEBC would lose its Philippine government franchise to operate.

Earlier in the day John Broger, who with Robert Bowman and William Roberts had founded FEBC, made a desperate plea for an extension of the deadline, but his petition had been denied. Government authorities had already granted FEBC a seven-week extension when the first completion date could not be met; they would yield no further. To retain its franchise, FEBC must be in operation by June 4.

Just three days before this final deadline something had gone wrong with one of the circuits. It had been repaired by June 4, but now there was no time to test the equipment. Wires were braided together and lying all over the floor. A tropical rain had drenched the transmitter building, which was still under construction and virtually roofless. Wives prayed constantly that their husbands working with high-voltage power lines in ankle-deep water would not be electrocuted. At 6:00 P.M. a switch was thrown and the transmitters hummed. DZAS was on the air. Two hours later the 1,000-watt transmitter kicked off from an overloaded circuit. But FEBC had given satisfactory proof of performance and retained its franchise.

This sputtering beginning in 1948 marked the start of gospel broadcasting in the Orient for FEBC, which today represents a vital means of reaching into China with the good news of Christ. FEBC broadcasts are now carried over four transmitters in the Philippines — two with 50,000 watts of power.

All of these stations — plus The Evangelical Alliance Mission's station HLKX in Korea and others — flash signals of faith across the Chinese mainland. For years there was little indication of their broadcasting effectiveness. But recently the strategic importance of these radio arms into China has been confirmed by refugees escaping the mainland. Two such expatriates, young athletes — one a boy, the other a girl — talked freely about religious life in China in an interview recorded by The Evangelical Alliance Mission's Radio Taiwan.

"Can you tell us how young people on the mainland find out about Christianity today?" an interviewer asked. "They have no churches to go to. They don't have any Bibles. Yet we hear that many of them, when they escape to Hong Kong, want to identify themselves with a Christian church. Can you tell us how this can be?"

"They no doubt heard about Christianity before they left the mainland," the girl replied. "They most likely listened to it on the radio."

"But how can you hear about Christianity on the radio when all you can listen to is Radio Peking?"

"Listening to Radio Peking makes no sense at all," was the boy's quick response. "You have to listen to other stations as well. That's how a lot of people on the mainland find out about Christianity today. You listen to any foreign station that carries a Chinese program. Secretly at night. Our family listened almost every night to a Christian station broadcasting from Manila."

"But you are too young," another interviewer persisted. "You cannot have heard about Christianity on the mainland. Didn't you hear about it after you got to Hong Kong?"

"I heard the gospel in my own home," the boy replied. "We listened to the Manila station to find out what was going on in the world."

"Do many people have radios on the mainland today?" he was asked.

"In our area quite a few people had them. It isn't the same in all places, however."

"Do people on the mainland know about the Christian radio stations?"

"Oh, yes," the boy answered. "In our area I knew a lot of people who used to listen. We could get only four foreign stations that carried Chinese programs. Since the Christian station in Manila was one of them, a lot of people listened to that station."

In Hong Kong as I talked with FEBC personnel and, later, with a TEAM Radio Taiwan representative, I gained insight into the frustrating ministry of shooting into the dark of China with radio beams.

"FEBC is really a faith ministry," I was told. "We don't know who is listening. Our Chinese staff faithfully prepares material day after day, only occasionally getting a letter from China, sometimes getting letters from only one person over a year's time. All we know for sure is that we merit periodic jamming. And we know the attitude of the Chinese government toward our radio broadcasts. It is illegal for Chinese citizens to listen to any broadcasts from outside their country. Now you can imagine, if that's illegal, the reprisals that would come against the people who might write to us, telling us that they were listening to our station."

Missionary Ed Torjesen, TEAM's U. S. representative for Radio Taiwan, outlined the meager history of response to Christian broadcasts: "For fifteen years we had only one letter. Then during the Cultural Revolution, when there was a complete breakdown of government control, we got nearly sixty letters from listeners in nearly every major part of China. From old Christians who thanked us for giving them the Word of God during this time when it was precious in the land. From young people who had been born and raised under Communism, whose main exposure to the gospel had been what they had heard over the radio. Now again letters are extremely rare. In 1972 we received only one, an innocuous response from a girl in Peking."

Lack of letter response does not daunt radio broadcasters, however. "The great thing that has happened as far as the Christian church is concerned," Torjesen told me, "is that even before we were aware of the deep darkness that would descend upon China, God had already begun to set up the channels by which he would communicate to that country. The Far East Broadcasting Company stations in Manila were designed to reach all of Southeast Asia, but one beam was aimed directly north into China when it was set up shortly after World War II. About the time of the Korean War TEAM was burdened to set up station HLKX in Korea with a beam also reaching into North China."

The Chinese programs carried by these stations are varied — music, drama, interviews, preaching, children's programs, English instruction, and Bible reading at dictation speed — all designed to gain the attention of the unknown mainland audience. The vital importance of radio in China's evangelization, however, is better understood within the context of the Chinese personality structure, which Ed Torjesen outlined for me.

The basic personality of the Chinese people has not changed for centuries, Torjesen believes. This can be seen when the Chinese come from the mainland into the free world. It is not long before they revert to their traditional responses. Yet the information coming out of Red China would indicate that something has changed. Obviously, there have been some very deep structural changes within the society which now affect the responses of the people. "While the people are still within this altered framework, we must find out what it is like so we can understand the responses of the people and communicate God's message to them in a way that makes sense in their situation," Torjesen explained. He listed several areas in which this change has been most pronounced.

One area is the relationship of the people to the land. "The Chinese people have always been very closely tied to the land," Torjesen pointed out. "For centuries, for generation after generation, the same family lived on the same piece of land. Even though they may not have owned the land, but were tenant farmers of rich landowners, still they lived on that piece of land, worshiped the spirits of their forefathers on that land, and tied their identity to that land. The Communists have successfully severed this connection between the individual and the land."

The upgrading of the status of the military constitutes another significant change. "The Chinese have despised the military for centuries. But the Communists needed the military both to impose and perpetuate their authority, so they had to upgrade its image. The result is that Communism, which professes to produce a classless society, has in fact produced a society that has an elite class, which is the military. The People's Liberation Army is everywhere."

The status of the intellectuals has also changed drastically. "The Chinese have traditionally looked up to the man of learning. However, Mao Tse-tung and the Communists distrust the man of independent learning, the man who thinks for himself. Therefore, in various stages, they launched a series of campaigns against intellectuals. Through these they not only downgraded the intellectuals but so humiliated and disgraced them that many committed suicide. Today one finds intellectuals in the Chinese countryside doing manual labor, in the communes, and in the production brigades."

Another area of change in China is the development of an outcaste class. If a person — or one of his relatives — belongs to one of the "five bad elements," he has no civil rights. The five bad elements are landowners, rich tenant farmers, counterrevolutionaries, persistent law breakers, and "rightists" in the Communists' way of thinking. A person in this class is considered a nonperson, without civil rights. "A large segment of the Chinese population are nonpersons,"

Torjesen told me. "They work under political supervision, sometimes in labor camps, and almost always at starvation wages. Eventually every one of these is to be liquidated, and the liquidation process is going on right now." Torjesen estimates that close to ten percent of the Chinese people fall into the category of nonpersons.

It can be a fearsome thing.

"You see your neighbor down the street and he's under political supervision and surveillance," Torjesen explained the nonperson's fear. "Then your neighbor disappears. You see it happen to another man, and you wonder why these people are getting unfair treatment. You see still another man go, a close friend of yours perhaps, and you begin to wonder, 'Am I also marked?' This may affect ardent Communists, too. Some have taken up to ten years to find out they were marked for extinction. There is no door open for them except death — or escape."

The family structure has likewise undergone a dramatic change. Realizing that China's cohesive family structures could provide a base for opposition and resistance to the government, the Communists set out to break family integrity. Mao Tse-tung's first ploy was the setting up of the commune system in 1956, when in addition to marshalling the total production of an area both agriculturally and industrially, he also imposed a fantastic social regimentation upon the people so that there were dormitories for men, separate ones for women, and yet separate places for children. The families of China were literally and physically pulled apart. Fortunately, the commune system failed and the families were allowed to get together again in production brigades, where a slightly modified economic system is pursued and where there is less social regimentation.

These radical changes have been devastating to society. "There has been a perversion of reality so that the everyday world one lives in is no longer his real world," Torjesen pointed out. "It is a contrived, artificial world. No one expects anyone to tell anything for the truth's sake because no one knows what the truth is. Everyone understands that people say what they say only because that is what they have to say in order to survive."

If their everyday world has become an artificial world, where then is their real world?

"It is the world of their dreams. The basic drive of a person in China today is how to survive as a person," Torjesen believes. "The Chinese people turn to their radios to find something with which they can identify, something which is not contrived, something which is real and true and free. They search for any station from outside of China that carries a Chinese program."

It is at this point that God meets them. Four of the eight or ten radio stations reaching China are Christian stations. There may be more people listening to the gospel on any one night in China today than at any other time in her previous history.

8 Wall Watching and Faith Praying

The young Chinese would have fit in easily with almost any group of today's idealistic youth. Like his peers around the world, he had become dissatisfied with an artificial lifestyle and had "turned on" to Jesus. His decision to accept Christ was unusual, perhaps, since it had been made in Communist China. He could not openly express his faith until he had escaped from his homeland. Shortly after his arrival in Hong Kong in May, 1971, the twenty-four-year-old refugee was asked about the situation for Christians in China. His surprising assessment was reported by the Lutheran World Federation Broadcasting Service:

"The young believers are really serious about their faith. If you are found out to be a Christian, though, you will be involved in some kind of trouble. You will be under observation. When we still had Sunday services — until 1965, when public worship was considered illegal — the church was always full. There were even people standing outside. People who did not have Bibles in their homes came early to pray and read the Bible."

"Did you have Bibles or other religious books at home?" he was asked.

"Some believers did. I took two to our village secretly. Most Christian families also had a hymnal in their homes. We always sang together whenever we gathered. We sometimes joined in singing hymns we heard on foreign broadcasts even though many of them were unfamiliar."

"Was there any opportunity for evangelism in China?"

"I found it was easy among young people. I myself led six to know God. It is my feeling that there are more Christians in China today than there were ten years ago."

Could there be more Christians in China today than ten years ago?

"Maybe yes . . . maybe no," concluded *Comment,* the monthly information paper published by World Vision's Asia Information Office, when it recorded the interview in its May 1972 issue.

Radio missionary Ed Torjesen asserts: "There is a very persistent feeling that there are more Christians in China today than there have ever been. While I have not been able to fully document this, nevertheless from my own interviews with people from China and from my own survey of the intelligence information that has come out I am convinced that this is possible. The increase in the number of Christian believers is found largely in China's frontier regions and her burgeoning labor camps."

The uncertainty about China's actual situation has allowed widely contradictory statements to be made without easy confirmation or refutation. In late 1971 an evangelical U. S. magazine quoted what it called "a China expert with fantastic knowledge of what's going on" as follows:

"Recently we conducted a survey which covered the whole country. Out of this has come a figure which is almost incredible. The general consensus is that about one in four hundred people in China has made some kind of profession of faith. In terms of the whole population, this works out to somewhere between two and two and one-half million. . . . In other words, since Communism came into power, the number of Christians in China has approximately doubled."

But a Chinese Christian leader told me this "expert" is a Westerner seeking to raise funds from Christian donors and that "few Chinese could agree with his estimate." According to this veteran observer, the magazine's glowing report of 250,000 New Testaments in the Mao-modernized script going through the bamboo wall is also wishful thinking — if not downright lying.

Other visitors to China give a pessimistic view of the church there. Ray and Rhea Whitehead, China scholars working in Hong Kong, were quoted in the February 6, 1972, *Lutheran Witness* after a tour of the People's Republic: "In our thirty days in China we met no Christians and saw no functioning Christian churches or Christian institutions. In some cities we saw church buildings which had been converted into factories or put to other use."

In the same report, however, the *Witness* also quoted Andrew Chiu, a pastor of the Lutheran Church — Missouri Synod Hong Kong Mission: "Through people coming out from the mainland we know there are still Christian churches there. . . . The Church, as the people of God, is still there."

Pastor Chiu went on to outline a practical program for evangelizing a segment of the Chinese population. "We must train our businessmen so that when they go on business to China, they can give their own witness. Second, we should emphasize radio and literature work because these will help to publicize the gospel among the Chinese. Third, the church in Hong Kong and Macao should work especially among the blue-collar workers and the laborers because these people can very easily go in and out of mainland China. If we have more Christians among them, we can expect them to witness among their relatives and friends when they visit."

Another innovative laic plan was suggested by Arthur F. Glasser, dean of the Fuller Theological Seminary School of World Missions, a former missionary to China and past U. S. home director of the Overseas Missionary Fellowship. "We should not limit God's Spirit to just using those people who have the same cultural background," he wrote in the January 1972 *Eternity*.

"There are already a lot of people who can go into China from Canada, from Europe, and from various other parts of the world. It seems to me that such contacts with Chinese Christians should be along the lines of men in the professions: engineers, diplomats, businessmen. In our day the church is increasingly shifting from a cleric dominated organism to a lay movement. This is especially true in countries where Communism is in power. So such contacts with Chinese Christians would be very healthy."

Along with the established effectiveness of radio outreach into China other methods of media evangelism are being attempted, particularly in the area of literature. In January 5, 1972, the *Alliance Witness* reported that a New Testament in the Mao-modernized Chinese language — a $75,-000 project of the American Bible Society, supported largely by the Assemblies of God — would be available in 1974. Underground Evangelism reported in July 1972 the preparation of a Chinese Youth Bible written in the modern simplified alphabet and using "terms that Chinese youth, raised in atheism, will both read and understand." UE said that, in association with Asian Outreach, its Gospel of Mark had already been published.

As the search for ways to penetrate China with the Christian message accelerates, most knowledgeable observers agree that the next attempt to reach that vast nation for Christ must not be a repetition of the hodgepodge of activity which characterized the 150-year mission history that ended abruptly in 1949.

Timothy Yu, considered to be one of the best-informed Christian China watchers, urges that the crusade for China be done cooperatively, utilizing the best talents of all mission groups. "No single mission can do the job thoroughly without facing financial or personnel difficulties," he emphasized to me. "My hope is that evangelical missions will try some way to form a general strategic plan together."

Yu would like to see a thorough analysis *now* of all publications coming out of China, of radio programs being broadcast there, and of refugees fleeing the mainland in order to determine the intellectual and philosophical status of today's Chinese — then plan literature and mass media programs to meet their needs.

Right now Yu is helping to train future Christian writers of the Orient through an innovative agency of communications in Hong Kong, which possesses modern radio, television, and press facilities. Yu senses the lateness of the hour. "The next twenty-five years should be a time of golden opportunity," he told me. "Either Christians take over or the Antichrist is going to."

Publisher Yu is the same seasoned watchman who told me that he could not see a dramatic change in current Chinese policy that would warrant optimism about a reopening of the country. Why then does he plan so ambitiously? Simply because he — and thousands of other concerned and praying Christians — put absolute trust in a sovereign God to ultimately meet the needs of the nation that accounts for a fourth of the world's population. Willing to await God's clear direction, he is nonetheless watchful and alert to opportunities for advance as they arise.

There is abundant proof that God has not forgotten China; he is surely as present there as elsewhere in his creation. God is still alive and well; he still responds to prayer. I learned much about praying from the imperturbable Chinese believers — so vastly different from Westerners who expect things to be accomplished immediately. When I shared my burden for China with one veteran laborer for Christ, he told me: "Faithful believers rest in God's wisdom. They do not question whether God will bring about a requested spiritual blessing — or even when he might do it. They just wonder how he will accomplish it so as not to stand in his way."

This must be our attitude toward the evangelization of China.

9 The Lamb and the Dragon

The eyes of the world turned eastward on a promising day in February 1972 to witness the impressive spectacle of an American President penetrating the awesome citadel of Communism known as China. Richard M. Nixon's mission for peace brought that mysterious land into American living rooms for scrutiny via television, radio, and the press. For years considered a fearsome foe bent on the supression of a free society and the destruction of all cultural and religious institutions, China suddenly became — if not an ally — at least a recognized and respected fellow nation. The famous "ping pong" diplomacy of 1971 wrought the long-sought opening of China — first to table tennis players, then to American journalists, and finally to the United States President. Yet, in spite of the intense scrutiny of her world neighbors, the nation remains an enigma.

China's guarded welcome to outside visitors barely exposes an internal strife that has always been a part of Mao's People's Republic. The atrocious Cultural Revolution of 1966-1968, for example, was the culmination of a long-standing power struggle between Mao and his chief of state, Liu Shao-chi. Mao suspected Liu of being untrue to his own brand of spartan Communism and thus permitting China to become corrupted like Russia by "revisionist" thinking. Mao encouraged young Red Guards to rampage against everything "bourgeois" and to purge Liu's supporters from key posts. When the youths got out of hand, Mao let the army restore order — but Mao's thoughts remained supreme.

In the fall of 1971, even as plans were being made for President Nixon's visit, China's internal unrest surfaced once again. According to *Time* magazine (October 4, 1971): "Almost the entire Politburo disappeared from public view from September 12 to September 16. A visiting Japanese delegation noticed an unusual amount of activity around the Communist Party headquarters in Peking, where lights were burning late into the night and many black sedans were parked outside. At the same time, the top military leaders dropped out of sight . . . . Air traffic over the mainland came to a near halt . . . . Military units were put on some sort of alert . . . . Obviously, something important had occurred in China . . . . Most China-watching experts focused their attention on the fate of Mao's heir-designate, Defense Minister and Vice Chairman Lin Piao, 65. Besides the fact that Lin is not physically robust, his political health may also be failing. He was closely identified with the excesses of the Great Prolitarian Cultural Revolution . . . . [Premier] Chou En-lai's position last week seemed by all accounts to be secure, if not enhanced."

The keenness of *Time's* guesswork was proven in late December when Peking diplomatic sources reported that Lin Piao had been "physically eliminated" and that Premier Chou En-lai had taken over as China's "political supremo." An interesting footnote was added to this terse announcement in early January, 1972, when Dev Murarka of the London *Observer* reported from Moscow:

"The Russians now are sure that Lin Piao, once deputy and heir to Chinese leader Mao Tse-tung, is dead. Medical experts, presumably Soviet and Mongolian, have reconstructed the charred remains of nine bullet-riddled bodies found in a Chinese aircraft that crashed in Soviet-dominated Mongolia last September. They had established with reasonable certainty that two of the bodies were those of Lin Piao and his second wife, Yeb Chun, though there seemed to be some misgivings that they could be doubles planted by Peking. According to information reaching Moscow and accepted as genuine, the former Chinese president, Liu Shao-chi, ousted at the beginning of the Cultural Revolution, also died in Peking some time in early November. Current Soviet thinking predicts trouble for the resilient Chinese Prime Minister, Chou En-lai. It is strongly suggested here that Mao will inevitably turn on Chou when seeking a scapegoat for recent or future failures."

It wasn't until the summer of 1972, however, that China came close to making a disclosure of what happened to Lin. He died September 12, 1971, in a plane crash in Mongolia, the Chinese embassy in Algiers announced, while he was fleeing China after an abortive attempt to assassinate Mao Tse-tung. Later Mao's niece, Deputy Foreign Minister Wang Hui-yung, confirmed the story in Peking.

While Mao controls the thoughts of many Chinese, his control over the nation of China is by no means harmonious. A British observer, a former missionary who spent many years in mainland China, told me: "I believe that Mao Tse-tung has the loyalty of certainly not more than five percent of the country. When Mao goes, there will surely be a revolution." And Mao, now in his eighties, can't live forever. That a sizable portion of China's 800 million citizens are dissatisfied with life can be seen most graphically in the number and regularity of defections from the People's Republic. The following two observations about the situation are significant.

In January 1972, World Vision's Asia Information Office *Comment* reported: "They keep coming into Hong Kong. They swim, float on inner tubes, stuff their pockets and pants with ping pong balls, and conceal themselves in the holds of Chinese junks."

Just seven months later, in August, Keyes Beech, reporting for the *Chicago Daily News* from

Hong Kong, revealed: "The Chinese Communists have cracked down hard on refugees who want to trade the spartan life of proletarian China for the mixed blessings of capitalist Hong Kong. The crackdown came the middle of last month, travelers from nearby Canton reported, but it did not stop 1,000 runaways from escaping to this British colony during July. This was the highest monthly total registered since the mass exodus of 1962 when 60,000 Chinese fled across the border because of famine conditions on the mainland. Nearly all the refugees are between seventeen and twenty-five years old. They also are physically fit. They have to be in order to run a gauntlet of Chinese troops, militia, and guard dogs before making a three-mile swim to Hong Kong."

China's new "open door" diplomacy is obviously intended to be only one way. Yet it represents an important change in policy. American and other Western newsmen are able now — after two decades of banishment — to stay in China and file regular reports to their news carriers. An increasing number of visitors are allowed to enter the country. What returning travelers and newsmen tell of their visits to China underscores the change that is taking place.

According to reporter Keyes Beech: "Travelers report there no longer is a picture of Mao in every hotel room. The *Little Red Book* of Mao's quotations — so lovingly compiled by Lin — is rapidly going out of circulation. Mao buttons have disappeared along with the Red Guards. There is a note of urgency in the campaign to rebuild the party structure that Mao destroyed. Technicians and managers have become respectable again after being chastised as a privileged group. The Chinese army, which restored order out of chaos when the Cultural Revolution got out of hand, is being put back in its place. Workers have been granted raises up to 25 percent, their first since 1964. Peasants have been assured they can keep their private plots and private pigs."

China is changing. Change for this mammoth dragon comes slowly, to be sure, yet surprisingly. During the year of the celebrated Presidential visit to China, significant and reliable reports on increased Christian activity reached the West. Ed Torjesen, Radio Taiwan representative, expressed optimism after attending a meeting of the "China group" mission leaders within the Evangelical and the Interdenominational Foreign Missions Associations. There Gordon Bell, Far East Broadcasting representative, and Don MacInnis, the National Council of Churches' chief China watcher, gave encouraging reports of open worship assembly in remote areas. "The incidents were far removed from Peking," Torjesen told me, "mostly in the Southwest. And also in Canton, which has traditionally been strongly independent. But they present a promising sign of boldness to witness." He pointed out that the worship was truly Christian and not the showcase compromise that is permitted in Peking.

In a report in *Eternity,* September, 1972, journalist Bell wrote: "While Richard Nixon crossed the snow-mantled square of the Old Imperial Palace in Peking last February . . . a small group of Christians gathered in a remote Chinese mountain village and worshiped Jesus, the God of all reality." Bell quoted a Christian young woman who had been sent to the countryside for "thought reform" and there stumbled upon a small group of Christian peasants. "Following Nixon's visit," she explained, "discipline became lax. Investigations were not as tight as before." According to Bell, "Though most Christians are not brave enough to meet openly, this girl's report adds to the impression of a growing restlessness in Mao's nation." The final statement he attributed to his informant is striking:

"Nobody knows what's going to happen tomorrow. Change [in China] always happens in an hour, a day, a week."

In his unique, redemptive fashion, the Lamb of God appears to be forcing open the door of the dragon's den.

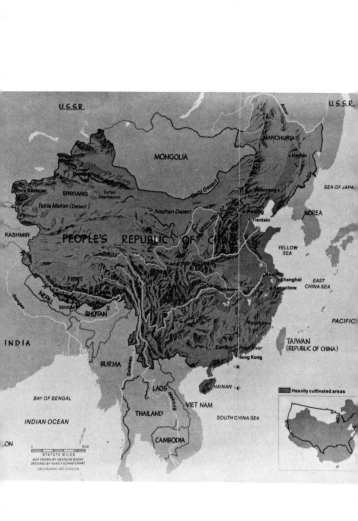

U.S.S.R.

U.S.S.R.

MONGOLIA

MANCHURIA

Harbin

Kashgar   SINKIANG   Turfan
                                Depression

Takla Makan (Desert)

Alashan Desert

Gobi Desert

Shenyang

Peking

Tientsin

SEA OF JAPAN

KOREA

KASHMIR

PEOPLE'S   REPUBLIC   OF   CHINA

YELLOW
SEA

TIBET

NEPAL

SIKKIM

BHUTAN

Ganges

Shanghai

Hangchow

Nanking

EAST
CHINA SEA

INDIA

PACIFIC

BURMA

Salween

Canton

Pearl River

Hong Kong

TAIWAN
(REPUBLIC OF CHINA)

BAY OF BENGAL

LAOS

Mekong

HAINAN

Heavily cultivated areas

INDIAN OCEAN

THAILAND

VIET NAM

SOUTH CHINA SEA

CAMBODIA

CEYLON

0   500
STATUTE MILES
MAP DRAWN BY ISKANDAR BADAY
DESIGNED BY NANCY SCHNEICKART
GEOGRAPHIC ART DIVISION

AFTERWORD

by Arthur Glasser
Dean, Fuller Theological Seminary
School of World Missions

Any Christian who is concerned about the Chinese people cannot but rejoice over the possibilities of new contact between America and China. The Chinese are too big a people, too central a people on the whole human stage, to be left out. Isolation from them is not in the world's best interest from the standpoint of peace nor in the church's best interest from the standpoint of witness and fellowship.

We cannot help but be concerned about the future of Taiwan. It is a temptation to view the events at the United Nations with unrestrained anger. We can point to the marvelous freedom for the gospel in Taiwan in contrast to the atheistic dictatorship in Red China — and wonder at the travesty of world justice that expels one and accepts the other.

Yet we know that God is sovereign. And we must remember that, while it is true that the gospel is flourishing in Taiwan, it is also true that the last five years of the missionary presence on the mainland were among the most fruitful years. God was greatly at work before the Communist take-over, yet in the mystery of his providence that door was closed to foreign presence there.

We can't play God here; we have to believe that he is in control. Our business is to respond creatively with words for the Christian Church in the face of the latest change. We have long had a burden for the Chinese people. Now, what are we going to do about it?